HOW AND WHY DO BIRDS FLY

SPEEDY
PUBLISHING

Speedy Publishing LLC
40 E. Main St. #1156
Newark, DE 19711
www.speedypublishing.com

Birds are a group of endothermic vertebrates, characterised by feathers, a beak with no teeth, the laying of hard-shelled eggs, a high metabolic rate, a four-chambered heart, and a lightweight but strong skeleton.

All animals need some kind of locomotion, or ability to move. Flight is the main mode of locomotion used by most of the world's bird species.

Birds have many physical features besides wings that work together to enable them to fly.

Birds have evolved many features to make flight possible. The skeleton is strong but light, with a large breastbone to support powerful muscles for flapping wings up and down.

The wings, are the key to bird flight. Birds have wings covered with feathers, which allow most of them to fly.

The wings themselves are curved on top, flatter beneath -air travels faster over the top surface of the wing reducing air pressure on the top of the wing and creating lift.

Larger wings produce greater lift than smaller wings. So smaller-winged birds need to fly faster to maintain the same lift as those with larger wings.

Feathers on a bird's wings provide a lightweight but solid surface to push against the air. A bird's feathers also keep them warm and dry.

When a bird is gliding, it doesn't have to do any work. The wings are held out to the side of the body and do not flap.

Birds' wings flap with an up-and-down motion. This propels them forward.

Some birds are small and can manipulate their wings and tail to manoeuvre easily.

Birds developed the ability to fly in order to adapt to their environment. Flight assists birds while feeding, breeding and avoiding predators.

Flying also allows them to escape nasty weather and migrate to warmer temperatures. Many species annually migrate great distances.

It is also used by some species to display during the breeding season and to reach safe isolated places for nesting.

Flight is more energetically expensive in larger birds, and many of the largest species fly by soaring and gliding as much as possible.

Printed in Great Britain
by Amazon

42485641R00021